OCD - Tools to Help Young People Fight Back!

by the same author

Breaking Free from OCD
A CBT Guide for Young People and Their Families
Jo Derisley, Isobel Heyman, Sarah Robinson and Cynthia Turner
ISBN 978 1 84310 574 9
eISBN 978 1 84642 799 2

of related interest

Understanding OCD
A Guide for Parents and Professionals
Edited by Adam B. Lewin and Eric A. Storch
ISBN 978 1 84905 783 7
eISBN 978 1 78450 026 9

Can I tell you about OCD?
A guide for friends, family and professionals
Amita Jassi
Illustrated by Sarah Hull
ISBN 978 1 84905 381 5
eISBN 978 0 85700 736 0
Part of the *Can I tell you about...?* series

Obsessive Compulsions
The OCD of Everyday Life
C. Thomas Gualtieri, MD
ISBN 978 1 78592 817 8
eISBN 978 1 78450 905 7

OCD – Tools to Help Young People
FIGHT BACK!
A CBT Manual for Therapists

Cynthia Turner, Georgina Krebs and Chloë Volz

Illustrated by Lisa Jo Robinson

Jessica Kingsley *Publishers*
London and Philadelphia

First published in 2019
by Jessica Kingsley Publishers
73 Collier Street
London N1 9BE, UK
and
400 Market Street, Suite 400
Philadelphia, PA 19106, USA

www.jkp.com

Copyright © Cynthia Turner and the South London and
Maudsley NHS Foundation Trust 2019
Illustrations copyright © Lisa Jo Robinson 2019

All rights reserved. No part of this publication may be reproduced in any
material form (including photocopying, storing in any medium by electronic
means or transmitting) without the written permission of the copyright owner
except in accordance with the provisions of the law or under terms of a licence
issued in the UK by the Copyright Licensing Agency Ltd. www.cla.co.uk or in
overseas territories by the relevant reproduction rights organisation, for details
see www.ifrro.org. Applications for the copyright owner's written permission to
reproduce any part of this publication should be addressed to the publisher.

Warning: The doing of an unauthorised act in relation to a copyright work may
result in both a civil claim for damages and criminal prosecution.

Library of Congress Cataloging in Publication Data
A CIP catalog record for this book is available from the Library of Congress

British Library Cataloguing in Publication Data
A CIP catalogue record for this book is available from the British Library

ISBN 978 1 84905 403 4
eISBN 978 0 85700 771 1

Printed and bound in the United States

Acknowledgements

There are many people who have contributed to the development of this programme. These include other professionals working in the field of childhood OCD, and many of the staff and trainees who have worked at the OCD, BDD and Related Disorders Clinic for Young People at the Maudsley Hospital. Special thanks to Isobel Heyman, who was central in helping to develop and refine many of the concepts and materials that are used here during her time as consultant psychiatrist of the OCD team at the Maudsley. We are very grateful to the therapists who were involved with our treatment trials using this workbook and manual, particularly Caroline Stokes, Holly Diamond, Jacinda Cadman and Amita Jassi. The more recent process of revising and updating these materials has truly been a team effort and in particular we would like to thank Benedetta Monzani for her many hours of work drafting new sheets and checking and cross-checking both publications. In addition, thanks go to Gazal Jones, Victoria Hallett and Angela Lewis for all their helpful hard work and contributions. Most importantly, we would like to thank the many children and families we have worked with who have contributed so much to our knowledge and understanding of OCD and its treatment.

Lastly, we would like to thank the funding bodies that have enabled us to test and refine this treatment manual and workbook. We are grateful to the Maudsley Charity, the National Institute for Health Research (NIHR) Patients Benefit (RfPB) Programme (grant reference number PB-PG-0107-12333) and the NIHR Maudsley Biomedical Research Centre grant for funding research trials that evaluated the effectiveness of this intervention. We are also grateful to the Medical Research Council who funded Georgina Krebs's Clinical Research Training Fellowship (reference number MR/N001400/1).

Research

This manual and workbook have been validated in a number of clinical trials. For further information, please refer to the following publications:

Turner, C., Heyman, I., Futh, A., and Lovell, K. (2009). 'A pilot study of telephone cognitive-behavioural therapy for obsessive-compulsive disorder in young people.' *Behavioural and Cognitive Psychotherapy*, 37(4), 469–474.

Turner, C. M., Mataix-Cols, D., Lovell, K., Krebs, G., Lang, K., Byford, S., and Heyman, I. (2014) 'Telephone cognitive-behavioural therapy for adolescents with obsessive-compulsive disorder: a randomized controlled non-inferiority trial.' *Journal of the American Academy of Child & Adolescent Psychiatry*, 53(12), 1298–1307.

Mataix-Cols, D., Turner, C., Monzani, B., Isomura, K., Murphy, C., Krebs, G., and Heyman, I. (2014). 'Cognitive–behavioural therapy with post-session D-cycloserine augmentation for paediatric obsessive–compulsive disorder: pilot randomised controlled trial.' *The British Journal of Psychiatry*, 204(1), 77–78.

Contents

Introduction	8
Overview of treatment	10
Cognitive behaviour therapy (CBT) for OCD family handout	12
Session 1: Learning about OCD and anxiety	13
Session 2: Learning to fight back: tools for beating OCD	19
Session 3: Learning to fight back: tools for beating OCD	23
Sessions 4–6: Continue fighting OCD using ERP	28
Session 7: Review progress	32
Sessions 8–12: Continue fighting OCD using ERP	34
Session 13: Completing ERP and overlearning in OCD	35
Session 14: Relapse prevention and end of weekly treatment sessions	37
Additional tools for fighting OCD	40
Follow-up Sessions 1–4	45

Introduction

This manual has been designed and written for use in treating young people with obsessive compulsive disorder (OCD). The treatment uses a type of therapy called cognitive behaviour therapy (or CBT). The primary CBT strategy employed in this programme is exposure and response prevention (ERP). In addition to ERP, this programme provides young people and their families with education about OCD and anxiety, and discusses relapse prevention and what to do if OCD should re-occur.

Before starting treatment, it is assumed that the young person has been assessed and diagnosed with OCD. As part of the pre-treatment assessment, we recommend using a validated OCD measure to gauge the severity of symptoms. This can then be re-administered later in order to track progress during treatment. The 'gold standard' measure for OCD in young people is the Children's Yale Brown Obsessive Compulsive Scale (CY-BOCS), which is a clinician-administered interview. If this is not feasible to administer, then a questionnaire measure can be used instead, such as the Children's Obsessive Compulsive Inventory (ChOCI), which comes in child- and parent-report versions.

This manual is produced in conjunction with a workbook that can be given to the young person and his or her family as a tool to help them integrate and follow up on what has been discussed.

Throughout this manual, the term young person is used to refer to both children and young people, and the term parent is used to refer to the young person's biological parent or step-parent or carer/guardian.

Typically, we work with young people of secondary school age but this manual and workbook can be used with children as young as six years old. With younger children, there would need to be more parental support and involvement.

Throughout the manual, reference is made to clinic-based therapy as well as to telephone therapy. This is because it was felt that the manual might serve the dual purpose of:

- supporting therapists in treating young people in clinic-based face-to-face therapy

- allowing therapists to develop confidence in treating young people via telephone CBT.

It was also envisaged that this manual might be useful in assisting clinicians in training to develop skills in treating OCD.

For clinic-based therapy, ideally both parents would be present for the therapy, but at least one parent/carer is required to attend sessions (flexibility is needed depending on the age and/or living circumstances of the young person).

The manual outlines the content of each session, and provides example text. This is primarily to assist therapists in training to gain experience and confidence in treating OCD in children and young people. For experienced therapists, the manual simply highlights the topic to be discussed with the young person, and the therapist should feel comfortable to hold a discussion with the young person using their own language and examples.

For telephone-based therapy, the majority of the session is conducted with the young person, and time with a parent is given at the end of the session. Allow 45–60 minutes for each session. Therapists are encouraged to time each session to assist in providing more precise time approximations for themselves in their ongoing use of this manual.

Before undertaking therapy, the therapist should explain to the young person that treatment sessions will be held each week, and that it will be necessary for the young person to practise tasks via completion of homework exercises in between sessions. Emphasise that there will be a team of people supporting the young person (i.e. therapist, family, etc.) and the whole team needs to make a commitment to beating OCD by attending the sessions, and by practising the things that they learn (just like learning new things at school).

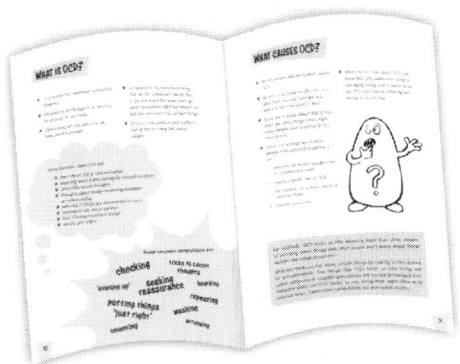

Example of OCD – Tools to Help You Fight Back! Workbook

A number of points that could be made repeatedly throughout the manual are presented here for the therapist's general awareness, and to limit repetition in the following pages.

- Throughout each session, the therapist should ensure that the young person fully understands everything that has been discussed.

- At the beginning of each session, the therapist should establish an agenda. Broadly speaking, the agenda for each session is:

    1. Review previous session and homework.
    2. Introduce new learning/tools for session.
    3. Ensure that the young person understands what is presented. For ERP tasks, understanding can best be facilitated with in-vivo practice in the clinic or with the therapist on the phone.
    4. Answer any questions with young person.
    5. Homework discussion for young person.
    6. Parent check-in.
    7. Answer any questions for parents.
    8. Homework discussion for parents.

- Ask the young person to take some time at the conclusion of the session to explain everything that has been discussed with their parent(s).

- Ask the young person to read through the relevant workbook pages for each week, and to write down any questions they have.

- Therapists should use their discretion with the amount of material covered in each session. If they feel it appropriate to work more quickly or more slowly than what is outlined in this manual, then they should do so. The guiding principle should be to ensure that the young person fully understands all topics and material presented, and that they develop confidence in overcoming OCD.

- The aim is to meet weekly for 14 sessions within 17 weeks, allowing a three-week leeway for holidays, illness and so on. Some young people may need more than 14 sessions to achieve a good recovery from their OCD. If they are not ready to finish at Session 14, we would recommend offering a further limited block of say seven more sessions and then review. We would only recommend offering further sessions if the young person is making progress – if not then treatment should stop and be reviewed and reconsidered.

- A note about autism spectrum disorder (ASD): OCD is extremely common among young people with ASD. Our research at the clinic demonstrates that young people with ASD can do well in treatment but that they may take longer to understand the underpinning of the model and may struggle to generalise their gains. The Maudsley Clinic is currently working on a modified treatment manual for this patient group. In the meantime, this manual can be used but it may be advisable to allow for up to 20 sessions and to take longer over the psychoeducation sessions.

- Feedback is welcomed from therapists who are working with this manual. Treating OCD in young people can tie us all up in knots! We hope that this manual and accompanying workbook will help you and the young person you are treating to make good progress fighting OCD. If anything was unclear or could have been done better, we would like to hear from you so that we can revise and improve this material when we get the opportunity. Please contact us with your feedback via either of the following email addresses: ocdbdd.camhs@slam.nhs.uk or cynthia.turner@uq.edu.au. We look forward to hearing from you!

The following points relate to the therapist's work with the parents, and again they are presented here for the therapist's general awareness, and to limit repetition in the following pages.

- If the young person is happy to discuss his/her OCD, ask parents to sit down and have a discussion with the young person after each session. Parents may be able to offer quite a lot of assistance to young people in their fight against OCD.

- Ask/remind parents to desist from giving advice to the young person about how he or she should manage the OCD. Parents should be encouraged to gently remind the young person what they have learned in therapy about fighting OCD. Therapists should discuss the best ways of parents doing this.

- Ask parents to praise their young person for times when they see that the young person is resisting the OCD, or fighting back against the OCD.

Overview of Treatment

- A maximum of 14 sessions are to be completed within 8–17 weeks

- Administer outcome measures at baseline, Session 14, three months, six months and 12 months follow-up.

Session 1: Learning about OCD and anxiety
- [ ] Establish rapport, e.g. young person's likes/dislikes
- [ ] Define and normalise obsessions and compulsions
- [ ] Discuss causes of OCD
- [ ] **Tool 1:** Externalising OCD
- [ ] **Tool 2:** Understanding anxiety (what is anxiety; fight or flight; anxiety rating scale; habituation)
- [ ] Set homework

Session 2: Learning to fight back
- [ ] Review Session 1 and homework
- [ ] **Tool 3:** Making an OCD hierarchy
- [ ] **Tool 4:** The OCD cycle
- [ ] What is CBT?
- [ ] Set up therapy goals
- [ ] Set homework

Session 3: Learning to fight back
- [ ] Review Session 2 and homework
- [ ] **Tool 5:** Exposure and response prevention
- [ ] **Tool 6:** Bossing back OCD using helpful thoughts
- [ ] Set homework ERP task

Session 4: Continue fighting OCD using ERP
- [ ] In-vivo ERP task: rate anxiety over time
- [ ] Set up ERP task for homework

Session 5: Continue fighting OCD using ERP
- [ ] In-vivo ERP task: rate anxiety over time
- [ ] Set up ERP task for homework

Session 6: Continue fighting OCD using ERP
- [ ] In-vivo ERP task: rate anxiety over time
- [ ] Set up ERP task for homework

Session 7: Continue fighting OCD using ERP
- [ ] In-vivo ERP task: rate anxiety over time
- [ ] Set up ERP task for homework
- [ ] Re-administer a measure of OCD

Session 8: Continue fighting OCD using ERP
- [ ] In-vivo ERP task: rate anxiety over time
- [ ] Set up ERP task for homework

Session 9: Continue fighting OCD using ERP
- [ ] In-vivo ERP task: rate anxiety over time
- [ ] Set up ERP task for homework

Session 10: Continue fighting OCD using ERP
- [ ] In-vivo ERP task: rate anxiety over time
- [ ] Set up ERP task for homework

Session 11: Continue fighting OCD using ERP

- [ ] In-vivo ERP task: rate anxiety over time
- [ ] Set up ERP task for homework

Session 12: Continue fighting OCD using ERP

- [ ] In-vivo ERP task: rate anxiety over time
- [ ] Set up ERP task for homework

Session 13: Completing ERP and overlearning in OCD

- [ ] Discuss overlearning
- [ ] In-vivo overlearning task: rate anxiety over time
- [ ] Set up overlearning task for homework

Session 14: Relapse prevention

- [ ] Review Session 13
- [ ] Think about future stressors
- [ ] **Tool 7:** A relapse prevention plan
- [ ] Think about future goals and plans
- [ ] Re-administer a measure of OCD

Follow-up sessions

at one month, three months, six months and 12 months post-treatment

F/U 1 date: one month post-treatment

F/U 2 date: three months post-treatment
Re-administer a measure of OCD

F/U 3 date: six months post-treatment
Re-administer a measure of OCD

F/U 4 date: 12 months post-treatment
Re-administer a measure of OCD

Additional tools

- [ ] **Tool 8:** Reassurance seeking and accommodation of OCD
- [ ] **Tool 9:** Normalising intrusive thoughts
- [ ] **Tool 10:** Learning to let thoughts go
- [ ] **Tool 11:** Responsibility pie charts
- [ ] **Tool 12:** Don't believe in OCD – find out for yourself

Cognitive Behaviour Therapy (CBT) for OCD Family Handout

You will be offered up to 14 sessions in 8–17 weeks (you may not need that many).

This treatment involves working with a therapist to fight your OCD through a step-by-step process. We aim to be flexible and collaborative in the way that we work with you, while at the same time sticking to an overall structure that we know works well.

Sessions 1–2	Education. This is where you and your family will learn more about OCD and how it works, and in particular the role that anxiety plays in keeping it going.
Sessions 3–6	Exposure and response prevention (ERP). After making a list of all the things that OCD makes you do (a hierarchy), you will then begin to try and stop, delay or mess up some of your rituals, with lots of help and support from your therapist and any family members who may be involved in helping. You may do some of these tasks at the clinic but you will also need to practise these every day at home.
Session 7	Review and measure OCD again.
Sessions 8–13	Continue fighting your OCD with regular ERP tasks both at the clinic and at home.
Session 14	Relapse prevention. We will work with you to make sure that you know what to do if OCD tries to come back.
Follow-up appointments	When you have finished your regular treatment, you will be offered four follow-up appointments over 12 months. These will be at one month, three months, six months and 12 months after treatment has ended.
Measurements	An important part of CBT is to measure the change that is taking place in order to see how you are progressing and how your recovery is impacting on your life and your family. You will have already completed initial measures and these will be repeated at Session 7 the end of your treatment, and again at three months, six months and 12 months after treatment.

A word about commitment to treatment...

We know that fighting OCD is tough and sometimes when you start fighting you can feel a bit worse before you feel better, but we are here to support you. Although you may not always feel like it, if you can attend every session and carry out daily tasks at home then you will make much quicker and better progress. Deciding to fight your OCD is a big commitment but it is worth it!

Session 1

LEARNING ABOUT OCD AND ANXIETY

For clinic-based therapy, ideally the whole family would be present for this session, or at least one parent/carer. For telephone-based therapy, the majority of the session is conducted with the young person, and time with a parent or carer is given at the end of the session.

> **PLAN FOR SESSION 1: Allow 60–90 minutes**
>
> 1. Establish rapport
> 2. Provide initial education about OCD: What is OCD?
> 3. Discuss causes of OCD
> 4. Introduce the young person to the tools that they will use for fighting OCD
>
>   **Tool 1:** Externalising OCD
>
>   **Tool 2:** Understanding anxiety (what is anxiety; fight or flight response; the anxiety rating scale; anxiety habituation)
>
> 5. Homework discussion for the young person
> 6. Parent check-in
> 7. Homework discussion for parents

1 Establish rapport

- **The therapist should spend some time at the start of the session getting to know the client.** The focus should not be on OCD, but instead on the interests of the young person. For example, likes and dislikes, special interests or hobbies, pets, friends, current activities, movies, videos.

- **Check the young person has the workbook** and what they have read and what they liked or disliked. It may be helpful to ask if they have done any previous therapy for OCD in order to ascertain what they may know about CBT already.

- **Establish an agenda for the session.** Explain to the young person that you are going to work together to try to understand what is going on with OCD. Take the young person through the structure of the session (i.e. the aim of this session is to get to know each other and to work in partnership to fight back against the OCD). Outline the planned agenda with the young person. (Refer to the 'Plan for Session 1' box above for agenda setting.) Ask the young person what they think of the agenda and check if they would like to add anything. Emphasise that if there is anything that they do not understand, or that they are unsure of, they should ask the therapist.

2 Provide initial education about OCD
(See workbook page 12)

- The manual conceptualises OCD according to a cognitive behaviour framework. This treatment programme is CBT using exposure and response prevention (ERP), which is the evidence-based treatment for OCD.

- **Emphasise to the young person/family that we are going to be working together to learn how to fight back against OCD** and reclaim their life. This helps to begin the process of externalising OCD, and helps to create a 'team' approach. As a way of introducing the model, explain that they are first going to learn more about OCD (with adolescents, it may be helpful to first ask what they know about OCD already, and use their existing knowledge as a basis for discussion).

- Provide an initial understanding of OCD by discussing: What is OCD? (See workbook page 12.)

- **Explain that OCD stands for obsessive compulsive disorder.**

- **Define obsessions** as unwanted thoughts, doubts, urges or images that typically make someone feel anxious or upset. Explain that sometimes in young people, the thoughts or obsessions might just be accompanied by a general feeling of discomfort. Some examples of obsessions are provided on page 12 of the workbook.

- Define compulsions as the actions or other things that we do to try and make the thoughts go away. That is, they are done to try to reduce the anxiety or to try to get rid of the uncomfortable feelings. Some examples of compulsions are provided on page 12 of the workbook.

- **Normalise obsessions and compulsions** by explaining that many of the symptoms of OCD are things that everyone thinks about, or does from time to time, but OCD makes us think about or do these things more often than other people do. Explain that OCD is normal anxiety gone wrong (i.e. the young person is not 'mad' or 'crazy').

3 Discuss causes of OCD
(See workbook page 13)

- **Emphasise that OCD is NOT a 'bad habit' or disobedience.**

- **Emphasise that OCD is nobody's fault.** It is a problem (just like asthma or diabetes, or even a broken leg) that must be treated and managed. Explain that OCD occurs in approximately one in every 100 young people. (Help to make this concrete for the young person by finding out how many people are in their school, and then thinking about how many students might have OCD.)

- Ask the young person what they think causes OCD, then work with their answer. Explain that nobody really knows what causes OCD, and discuss that there are currently several different explanations. Give a few examples, such as:
  - worrying too much if you get a bad or unpleasant thought
  - having a family 'risk' of OCD. This usually means that there is someone else in your family who has had OCD
  - having low levels of a brain chemical called serotonin, which has been found to play an important role in OCD
  - having stressful things which are happening or have happened in your life.

- Finish this discussion by suggesting that we simply don't know at this stage what the cause is, and it may well be that there are multiple causative factors. Emphasise, however, that **the most important thing is that CBT has been shown to be the most effective psychological treatment in helping young people overcome OCD.**

4 Introduce the young person to the tools that they will use for fighting OCD
(See workbook pages 14-21)

Tool 1: Externalising OCD

- The process of externalising OCD involves helping the young person (and parents) to learn to see OCD as a problem that is separate from the young person. That is, it is a problem that must be overcome. Unfortunately, many young people can think that OCD thoughts represent their own thoughts. Similarly, parents may sometimes think that obsessions and compulsions represent a young person's desired thoughts or behaviours, which can lead to blame and anger towards the young person. This is not so.

- It can be helpful for some young people to externalise OCD by giving it a name, or by drawing a picture of OCD (workbook page 14). This process of externalising OCD is a narrative technique that was first incorporated into young person OCD treatment protocols by Dr John March and colleagues. Calling OCD by its name (or nickname) helps everyone to understand that it is a separate problem from the young person. Give young people the opportunity to draw OCD if they would like to (either in the session or for homework), but emphasise that drawing or naming it is optional.

- For older children or adolescents, OCD can be more simply externalised by the language that the therapist uses. For example, by referring to OCD as an entity in its own right, in phrases such as 'What is the OCD telling you to do now?', 'What would OCD want you to do in that situation?' This externalising language should be maintained throughout.

- Some families may need additional encouragement to see OCD as external to the young person, if they have got very used to blaming him/her for their behaviours.

Tool 2: Understanding anxiety (what is anxiety; flight or fight response; the anxiety rating scale; anxiety habituation)

- Use a whiteboard or the workbook to assist in this discussion. **Ask the young person what anxiety means to them.** Determine what language they use to describe anxiety (e.g. feeling scared, feeling wobbly, feeling weird or strange).

- **Explain that it is important to understand anxiety, because anxiety is one of the main things that keeps OCD going.**

- **Describe anxiety as a normal feeling** that everyone gets from time to time. Ask the young person to give some examples from their everyday life (i.e. not OCD) of times when they feel anxious (e.g. giving a talk in front of the class, being introduced to a new person, being scared of dogs). It might help for the therapist also to give some examples of situations that usually cause them to feel anxious.

- Explain that anxiety is an emotion or feeling that involves certain thoughts and physical sensations. Use the workbook (page 15) or the board to draw the outline of a person and ask the young person to identify **what type of anxiety symptoms they get** (e.g. racing heart, upset tummy, sweaty hands, feeling shaky). Younger people can illustrate where on their body they feel anxious. What sort of thoughts do they have when they feel anxious? Typically, thoughts are about harm or danger to ourselves or to those we love. Normalise all symptoms of anxiety, both thoughts and physical sensations.

- Emphasise that **anxiety can't hurt us!** Although anxiety may feel unpleasant, it cannot do any harm.

- Discuss the role of **anxiety as a helpful response** (see page 16 of the workbook). Anxiety has a role in helping to protect us and keep us safe from harm or danger. This is known as the **flight or fight response**. When we are faced with a very real, dangerous situation or threat, our body prepares to help us to stand and fight, or to run away (flight). Our brain registers the threat, and the body's (sympathetic) nervous system is activated. A chemical called adrenalin (epinephrine) is released. A muscular response ensures that we can run from the danger or face it. Typical responses include:

  - acceleration of heart and lung action (increased breathing and heart rate)
  - inhibition of stomach and intestinal activity (butterflies or nausea)
  - constriction of blood vessels in some body parts (feeling faint or dizzy)
  - dilation of blood vessels in muscles (shaky)
  - inhibition of tears and salivation (dry mouth or eyes)
  - relaxation of bladder (need to go to the toilet).

- Many animals and all humans demonstrate this flight or fight response (anxiety) when faced with danger, and it is adaptive and helpful. For example, in an African grassland, a zebra that sees a lion racing toward him immediately bounds away as a result of this muscular activation (sympathetic nervous system). Similarly, in a more urban setting, a cat might flee from a dog. If the cat could not flee (e.g. being cornered in a room), the fight response would begin. There are also many examples of this response seen in humans. In movies about war, an army faced with an enemy illustrates both the fight and flight response. If faced with a larger army, they may flee, but if their road to safety were blocked by the same attacking army, they would fight. Our body's biological response is designed to help us in these circumstances.

- The fight or flight system is so important, and essential to our survival, that it sometimes kicks in when there is no real danger or threat. For example, if we stand on the garden hose when it is dark outside and we can't see what we have stood on, our immediate thought might be one of danger (e.g. a snake) and we might run inside to safety. However, once we realise that there is no real danger, and it is just the garden hose, the anxiety will come down. A similar example might be the noise made by a household cat in the night, or by a family member getting up to go to the bathroom in the night. This illustrates how a thought can trigger our anxiety, even if there is no real danger.

Anxiety rating scale

- Explain that some things cause us to feel more anxious than others. Use the **anxiety rating scale** (workbook page 17) to illustrate this. Explain that a 0 on the scale would be a completely relaxed feeling (like watching TV or reading a book you enjoy), whereas a 10 on the scale would be feeling really, really scared – as scared as you could ever imagine feeling (e.g. fearing that a loved one will die, someone pulling a gun on you in the street, jumping out of a plane and your parachute not opening). Explain that at a level 10, other people would clearly see and know you're anxious (e.g. you'd be shaking, crying, pacing, shouting).

- Help the young person to think about some of the different things in their life (not OCD) that they feel anxious about. **Help the young person to use the rating scale by giving an anxiety rating to some of the situations they identified** make them feel anxious (workbook page 18). Encourage them to think of as many **non-OCD anxiety-provoking situations** as they can and to practise using the rating scale to rate these examples. **This can be finished for homework if there is not enough time within the session.**

Anxiety habituation

- **Select an example of a non-OCD anxiety to illustrate the principle of anxiety habituation** (workbook page 19).

- Explain that habituation is a word used to describe the process of 'getting used to' something. Commonly cited examples are the processes of habituating to cold water or to loud noise; for example, when we first jump into a cold pool, we feel cold all over, but our body quickly becomes accustomed to the temperature, resulting in us not feeling so cold any more. Similarly, on first encountering very loud noise (e.g. trains going by), we may feel overwhelmed, but if we are exposed to that noise for long enough (e.g. live near a train station) then we adjust or habituate to the noise.

- Similarly with feelings of anxiety, when we first encounter an anxiety-provoking situation, our anxiety quickly reaches an uncomfortable level, and our flight or fight response kicks in. However, if we remain in the situation, our anxiety will begin to drop down on its own. Consider the example of performing in a school play. On opening night, our anxiety is at its peak, but as the play goes on, our anxiety begins to drop away. Illustrate this on a graph (using a 0–10 anxiety scale on the y-axis).

- If we continue to encounter the same anxiety-provoking situation over and again (e.g. perform the play every night for several consecutive nights), then on the second night, our anxiety will rise, but not quite as high as the first night. On the third night, our anxiety will rise again, but not as high as on previous nights, and will drop away again. This process will continue until we feel very little anxiety about performing at all. Again, illustrate this on a graph (using a 0–10 anxiety scale on the y-axis).

- Explain that when we do a compulsion, the anxiety comes down quickly. However, what we also know is that OCD will demand more and more compulsions to bring the anxiety down. It is important, therefore, to emphasise that compulsions become less effective, and as we know anxiety will come down even without doing a ritual, the more we practise **not** doing a ritual the more anxiety comes down.

- Check with the young person that they understand this process. For instance, you could ask them to explain it back to you.

5 Homework discussion for young person
(See workbook page 23)

- To facilitate and consolidate the learning, we recommend the young person reads over Session 1 before the next session.

- **If the young person was unable to come up with a name for OCD during the session, ask them if they would like to think of a name for homework** (and for younger people, maybe draw a picture of OCD). For older adolescents, you may simply decide to use 'OCD' as a name.

- Ask the young person to practise noticing anxiety and **continue with the anxiety rating scale**, generating non-OCD things that make them feel anxious, and then rating how anxious they would feel about doing these things.

- **Ask the young person to pay particular attention to times during the week when they have successfully been the 'boss' of OCD**, and not done what OCD wanted them to do (see workbook page 22).

- Finally, the therapist should **ask the young person if they have any questions about the session. Ask the young person for clear feedback about the session** (i.e. if they understood everything, if they didn't like anything or didn't agree with anything). Also ask the young person to write three things that they learned from Session 1 for homework and encourage them to write any questions they may have over the course of the week so that these can be addressed in the next session.

- **Discuss with the young person that you are now going to talk to their parent/carer.** Check if there is anything that the young person would like to keep confidential from their parent/carer (the therapist should use their own clinical judgement to determine what should be kept confidential and what possibly should not be).

- Also ask the young person to give some thought to how their parent/carer could assist with the homework.

 Remember to make the next appointment time with the young person.

6 Parent check-in

- If parents have been present during the session (as opposed to telephone treatment), adapt the instructions accordingly.

- At this point, it is helpful for the **therapist to introduce himself or herself to the young person's parents**. Ask parents if there is anything that they would like to know about the therapist (e.g. have they worked with this problem before, what qualifications they have).

- **Ask parents if they have read any background materials that were provided** (if relevant). Answer any questions that parents may have about things they have read.

- **Check with parents their understanding of what OCD is**, what causes and maintains it, and what anxiety is. Parents should be given the same information/education about OCD and anxiety that the young person was in this session. Where possible, young people should be encouraged to discuss this with parents to ensure that the young person fully understands. Therapists can then be on hand to correct any misinformation. It may be helpful for parents themselves to have a copy of the young person's workbook, and be able to draw on their reading materials to facilitate and progress through this discussion quite quickly.

- Explain that **parents do have an important role to play in assisting the young person**, and that role will be discussed more and more as treatment progresses. For the time being, ask parents to desist from giving advice to the young person about how they should manage the OCD. Also ask parents to help the young person at this point by encouraging them to complete their homework. If parents are involved in the young person's rituals, ask parents to continue with the OCD as they have been for now. Reassure parents that this is one aspect of OCD which will be discussed in treatment; however, at this early stage, it is best to simply continue with what the family has been doing.

- **Give parents the opportunity to ask any questions** that they may have about OCD or about the treatment that will be undertaken.

7 Homework discussion for parents

- **Ask the parents to pay particular attention to some of the strengths the young person displays** (i.e. things that they do well). Suggest that these might seem like small things to some people, but when life has been bossed by OCD for a long time, these are in fact big achievements.

- Ask parents to pay particular attention to times during the week when their young person has successfully been the 'boss' of OCD.

- If the young person is happy to discuss their OCD, **ask parents to sit down and have a discussion with them about Session 1**.

 Remember to check that the next appointment time is suitable for them.

Session 2

LEARNING TO FIGHT BACK: TOOLS FOR BEATING OCD

> **PLAN FOR SESSION 2: Allow 45–60 minutes**
>
> 1. Review Session 1, including Tools 1 and 2
> 2. Review Session 1 homework
> 3. Introduce the young person to the next tools that they will use for fighting OCD
>   **Tool 3:** Making an OCD hierarchy
>   **Tool 4:** The OCD cycle
> 4. Provide an overview of the CBT treatment that the young person is about to undertake, including a discussion of ERP
> 5. Setting goals for therapy
> 6. Homework discussion for young person
> 7. Parent check-in
> 8. Homework discussion for parents

1 Review Session 1, including Tools 1 and 2

- The therapist should spend some time at the start of the session **reviewing the content of the previous session** (Tools 1 and 2), and checking that the young person understood all that was discussed. This recap is in the young person's workbook. See guidance notes in the introductory session.

2 Review Session 1 homework

- Check that the young person now has a name for OCD, if they have chosen to give it a name. Ask whether the young person was able to **recall an example of when they were able to resist (fully or partially) doing something that OCD wanted them to do.**

- The therapist should spend some time going through the **young person's anxiety rating task** to ensure that both young person and therapist have a shared understanding of what anxiety is, how it feels in the body, and of rating anxiety.

3 Introduce the young person to the next tools that they will use for fighting OCD

(See workbook pages 27-36)

Tool 3: Making an OCD hierarchy

- **Introduce Tool 3: Making an OCD hierarchy** (workbook pages 27–29). Use the assessment information (e.g. CY-BOCS) to help the young person begin to develop a target list of OCD symptoms. It is easiest to focus on building a list of compulsions, or things that OCD makes the young person do.

- Ask the young person to brainstorm as many compulsions as they can think of. Ensure that this includes **avoidance behaviours, or things**

the young person is NOT doing, but should be doing given their age and developmental stage.

- In helping the young person construct this list, **check carefully for hidden or covert mental rituals**, such as prayers, 'cancelling out', special words or numbers or phrases, good thoughts, or pictures in their minds.

- Also ask about **'just right' phenomenology**. Some young people report that they have to do something until it feels just right, for example scratching, touching, evening or straightening things.

- Last, ask the young person also to **list things that other people** (e.g. family members, teachers, friends) **have to do for OCD**. This may include answering questions when the young person is seeking reassurance. If the young person and family recognise that this is a major issue for them then they may find it helpful to look at Tool 8: Reassurance seeking and accommodation of OCD (see pages 112–113 of workbook and pages 40–41 of this manual).

- **For a very small minority of young people, OCD is experienced as obsessions only.** (See workbook pages 114–119 to know more about how to tackle obsessions in OCD.) If this is the case, ask the young person to begin to develop a list of obsessions that they experience. Try to encourage the young person to identify a trigger for their obsessions. However, it is important to always check for the existence of compulsions by asking them to carefully think about the things they may do because of the obsessions. Check carefully for covert mental rituals that the young person may do to neutralise or 'cancel out' the obsession. It is more common that an obsession will be neutralised by a covert ritual rather than being an 'obsession only'.

- It is unlikely that the young person will be able to recall all symptoms at this time. Positively reinforce the young person for their efforts, and **explain that this list will be used throughout therapy**. It is therefore something that the young person will be asked to look at each week for homework until both young person and therapist are sure that they have a complete list of compulsions.

- Now it is time to help the young person review their list and **develop an OCD symptom hierarchy**. This is easiest to do if you use a whiteboard or the workbook (page 27). It involves using the anxiety rating scale introduced previously. For each compulsion identified in the OCD list, ask the young person to provide an anxiety rating (using the anxiety rating scale). The most important thing to remember is that **the anxiety rating is done by considering how hard (i.e. how anxiety-provoking) it would be for the young person to resist doing the compulsion (or to not avoid something they have been avoiding)**.

- Once all compulsions have been assigned an anxiety rating, ask the young person to put them into rank order, from the least anxiety-provoking compulsion to resist to the hardest one to resist (see workbook page 29).

- The therapist may like to continue this task in session, or to ensure the young person understands what is required, have the young person complete the task for homework. Please be aware that some young people might report compulsions as 10 out of 10 anxiety and may need more time to work on this.

Tool 4: The OCD cycle

- Another important tool for fighting OCD is **understanding how OCD works**. It is useful then to move on to the idea that OCD can be thought of as a vicious 'OCD cycle' (see page 31 of the workbook).

- Using the diagram illustrating how OCD works (page 31), highlight that OCD is a problem that affects our thoughts, feelings and behaviour.

- **Link the thought, feeling and behaviour boxes to the OCD symptoms that the young person is presenting with, and then encourage them to come up with a second example of their own.** If the young person is clearly able to understand the link between obsessions, anxiety and compulsions (or avoidance), discuss the idea that giving in to OCD by performing compulsions or avoiding the feared object or situation just makes the OCD stronger the next time.

- **Ask the young person if they feel this model fits with their experience**, and then ask them to think of other examples of their own (see workbook page 32).

- **Ask the young person to consider where, and how, they would break the cycle.** Use their answer to work through the cycle and **explain**

the principle of ERP. Ensure that the young person understands that they can break the cycle by changing their behaviour. Breaking the vicious cycle is about making them stronger and OCD weaker. Every time you break the cycle, you win, and OCD is made weaker. If you avoid or ritualise, you give in, and OCD is made stronger. The therapist may like to refer back to the anxiety curves on pages 19–21 of the workbook at this point to explain that through doing regular ERP tasks, anxiety will decrease.

- Highlight for the young person that **they have just been thinking about one of the key strategies for overcoming OCD using CBT, that is, exposure and response prevention (ERP)**.

- Use this discussion to then move on to talk about CBT.

4 Provide an overview of the treatment that the young person is about to undertake, by discussing CBT and ERP

(See workbook page 37)

It is important to **provide a framework for helping the young person to understand the treatment they are undertaking**. The following points relate to engaging the young person in a discussion about CBT and its role in overcoming OCD.

- **Explain that CBT stands for cognitive behaviour therapy.** CBT will involve the young person (and family) learning a number of tools that will help them to fight the OCD, and win back control over their thoughts and behaviour. It is called cognitive behaviour therapy, because the tools that we use to fight the OCD are 'thinking tools' (cognitions) and 'action tools' (behaviours).

- Explain that CBT is an **active treatment**.

- It will involve attending **regular sessions with homework** in between sessions.

- Provide an opportunity for the young person to answer any questions they may have about CBT.

- Normalise for the young person any anxiety they feel (if relevant) at the idea of CBT and ERP. Emphasise that **treatment will progress at the young person's pace**, taking small steps at a time, the only rule being that we must move forward in the fight. **Explain that ERP is graded** (i.e. starts with something the young person can manage), **prolonged** (until anxiety decreases) and **repeated** (e.g. over and again until it becomes easier and less anxiety-provoking).

- It may be helpful to briefly remind the young person of the anxiety curves (i.e. how anxiety works). Review the idea that when we feel anxious about something (e.g. doing an OCD task) the anxiety is initially high, but it passes when we learn that there is nothing to feel frightened of. If we keep on doing the thing that we felt anxious about, the anxiety becomes smaller and smaller each time.

- Help the young person to understand how **OCD is controlling them and the family at the moment, by bossing them into doing things that they do not want to do.** Use examples of the young person's symptoms to illustrate this.

- CBT treatment may or may not be undertaken in conjunction with medication. **If medication has been prescribed, explain the role that medication plays** in helping to get the young person 'ready' to fight/boss back the OCD. For example, some therapists like to use American psychiatrist Jeffrey Schwartz's analogy of using medication as 'arm-bands' to make it easier for the young person to learn the skills that will help them to 'fight back' against the OCD. That is, using arm-bands makes it easier for a young person to learn a new skill (swimming), but once learned, the skill is practised without arm-bands and the young person's confidence in his or her ability then continues to grow. Similarly with medication, the young person must still learn the skills they will need to overcome OCD, but medication may make this a little easier and less anxiety-provoking for them initially.

- Explain to the young person that fighting back against OCD is sometimes going to be really hard work, but that the young person is not alone. Emphasise that **the young person is supported by a team of people, and the team will work together to beat the OCD.**

- Explain that **the next steps will involve fighting the OCD by using ERP.** Link this to the homework task of last week if the young person was able to identify an example of partially or fully resisting OCD.

5 Setting goals for therapy
(See workbook page 38)

- Having goals helps set the direction for the treatment and can also be used to measure the young person's progress throughout the treatment.

- Discussion around goals can include the 'magic wand' question – that is, asking the young person what life would look like and what they would be doing differently if they woke up one day and found that all their problems were solved.

- Goals should be **S**pecific, **M**easurable, **A**chievable, **R**ealistic, **T**ime-defined – SMART. The therapist should also consider what skills, support or help the young person needs in order to successfully achieve goals.

6 Homework discussion for young person
(See workbook page 39)

- Encourage the young person to read over Session 2 before the next session.

- If the **OCD hierarchy** was not completed within the session, it would be helpful for the young person to continue with this task for homework.

- Ask the young person to complete the therapy goals worksheet (page 38), generating goals they would like to achieve by the middle and end of treatment.

- It is important the young person **understands the links between obsessions, anxiety and compulsions** (or avoidance), so ask them to come up with more examples of their OCD and practise completing the OCD cycle worksheets (pages 34–36).

- Finally, as homework, the therapist should ask the young person to write three things learned in Session 2, and any questions they may have over the course of the week, which can be addressed in the next session.

Remember to make the next appointment time with the young person.

7 Parent check-in

- The therapist should briefly **review the content of the previous session** with parents, and their homework tasks. Briefly **explain to parents what has been discussed with the young person** (or if clinic-based, ask the young person to briefly explain to parents the content of the session).

- **Give parents the opportunity to ask any questions** that they may have about the session content (or about OCD in general).

8 Homework discussion for parents

- **Ask parents to praise the young person for times when they see that the young person is resisting the OCD.** Descriptive praise is most effective, and remind parents that descriptive praise specifically describes what it is the young person has done, and how the parent feels about it. For example, 'I noticed that you only showered today for 28 minutes instead of 30 minutes! I feel really proud of you for the effort you are putting into fighting the OCD.'

- OPTIONAL: If parents/therapists are open to the idea of giving rewards to the young person for the efforts they are putting in, suggest that parents may like to sit down with their young person and **brainstorm a list of rewards** that they could give the young person as extra special encouragement for the fight against OCD. Suggest to parents that they look at rewards that are pleasurable but not expensive (e.g. a favourite dinner, choosing a movie, inviting a friend over). Ensure that parents understand that rewards are things that the young person will find motivating, not things that the parents think the young person might find motivating.

Remember to check with parents that the next appointment time is suitable for them.

Session 3

LEARNING TO FIGHT BACK: TOOLS FOR BEATING OCD

> **PLAN FOR SESSION 3: Allow 45–60 minutes**
>
> 1. Recap what the young person has learned so far in Sessions 1 and 2
> 2. Review Session 2 homework
> 3. Introduce the young person to the next tools that they will use for fighting OCD
>   - **Tool 5:** Exposure and response prevention
>   - **Tool 6:** Bossing back OCD using helpful thoughts
> 4. Homework discussion for young person: Fighting back! Putting ERP into action
> 5. Parent check-in and homework discussion for parents

1 Review Sessions 1 and 2

- The therapist should spend some time at the start of the session **reviewing the content of the previous sessions** (including a review of Tools 1–4), and checking that the young person fully understood what was discussed previously. The young person should be able to demonstrate understanding of anxiety and OCD, and of CBT (including ERP).

- Ask the young person if they had any questions regarding the content of the previous session.

2 Review Session 2 homework

- The therapist should **review the OCD hierarchy** that the young person was asked to complete for homework. If telephone therapy is being conducted, the therapist would benefit from taking notes on these pieces of homework. The therapist should spend some time on this review to ensure that the young person was able to accurately list and rate and rank order compulsions (and obsessions if this was done). Check the ratings given by asking the young person if it would be harder to stop symptom A than symptom B. Would it be harder to stop symptom B than symptom C? And so on.

- If the young person has had difficulty in identifying compulsions or obsessions, the therapist may also like to use some additional questioning to help the young person to elicit this information, such as:
  - What would you do if…?
  - How would you do…?
  - Is there a special order you use in doing that, or is there a special way you have of doing that?
  - What would you do then?
  - Is that everything?
  - Do you need someone else to help you do anything?
  - Do you need to do anything in a certain order or in a special way?

- If the young person is having difficulty identifying obsessions, and the therapist would find information about obsessions helpful, downward arrow questioning can be helpful to **assist in trying to elicit the core fears held by the young person**. For example, if the young person is only able to identify a feeling of discomfort, the therapist should question the young person around what the OCD would say or do if the young person actually touched the trigger.

The following questions may assist:

- What would be so bad about that?
- What would happen then?
- Why would that be so bad?
- If that did happen, why would that be so awful?

The therapist should use these and other questions to help the young person fill out the symptom picture as clearly as possible. If the process of questioning fails to elicit an identifiable fear, the therapist should help the young person rate the compulsion or the 'just right' feeling that exists.

3. Introduce the young person to the next tools they will use for fighting OCD

(See workbook pages 43-46)

Tool 5: Exposure and response prevention
(See workbook page 43)

- The therapist should follow up on last week's discussion of the principles of ERP by suggesting to the young person that it would be a good time now to pick a small part of OCD to fight back against. **Check that the young person fully understands the concepts of exposure (facing the fear) and response prevention (fighting the action), and of how ERP works (i.e. anxiety curves).** Remind the young person that the first time we face the fear, we feel anxious or scared. Explain that if we *avoid* or do a *ritual*, this prevents us from learning that nothing bad will really happen. It also makes the anxiety/OCD stronger the next time we are in that situation and strengthens the belief that the only way to cope is to avoid or to do the ritual.

- Remember to **reinforce that ERP will progress at the young person's pace**, but that together, you are going to fight the OCD one step at a time. It might be possible to use examples from previous homework of how the young person has already begun to fight back against the OCD and resist some of the things that OCD tries to make him/her do.

- **Ask the young person to think of a 'fighting back' task that they think they could manage** (however small). The therapist's role is to try to collaborate with the young person in selecting a task. The symptom hierarchy developed in the last session should help in now selecting a task. Encourage the young person to select a fear and related compulsion from somewhere towards the bottom of their list. Tips for choosing the first ERP task are included in the workbook on page 43.

- If all obsessions and compulsions were rated as extremely high, the therapist should work with the young person to **break down a fear into smaller steps**. For example, if the young person notes that they always avoid the window for fear of being contaminated by germs (therefore rating the fear as a 10), ask how fearful the young person would be if they touched an object that was located next to the window sill, or an object that sat on the window sill. Brainstorm possible ERP targets that are related to the fear, but not as difficult as the target identified by the young person.

- **Use the worksheet on page 43**, and ask the young person to identify what OCD is telling them to do (i.e. clearly identify the fear and the associated ritual/avoidance). Then ask the young person to identify what their fighting back experiment is going to be (i.e. their ERP task). Third, ask the young person to rate how anxious they feel about *not* doing what OCD would like them to do (using the rating scale introduced earlier in the session).

- **The therapist should then encourage the young person to 'face the fear' and 'fight the action' with them in the session** (on the other end of the telephone). If necessary, the therapist may need to model the task for the young person first. When doing the ERP task, the therapist should provide plenty of reinforcement, support and praise. The therapist should help and prompt the young person to monitor their anxiety levels every few minutes. Explain that the young person must continue with the ERP activity until the anxiety has significantly decreased. (Anxiety ratings at least halved is a good rule of thumb for then ceasing an ERP task, although the therapist may like to continue for a little longer if they feel that continued exposure would result in lower anxiety ratings.)

- **The therapist should work with the young person to map out their anxiety ratings using the model of anxiety curves discussed previously** (i.e. demonstrate using the whiteboard or a piece of paper that the anxiety curve process actually does happen).

- **Help the young person to complete the ERP worksheet and associated anxiety monitoring form** (workbook pages 43–44). These forms will be the young person's ongoing guide for completing ERP tasks.

- Note: in setting up an ERP task, **specificity is the key.** Be as precise as possible about what is actually going to be done.

THERAPIST NOTE

Remind the young person that it is important *not* to engage in any rituals (overt or covert), or any avoidance or neutralising behaviours while doing an ERP task. It is also important to ensure that the young person does not compensate for doing the ERP task by doing extra rituals later (e.g. extra handwashing to feel clean again after doing an exposure task).

Tool 6: Helpful thoughts
(See workbook pages 45-46)

- Explain to the young person that OCD makes us worry about a lot of things by using some sneaky tricks on us. OCD is especially good at tricking our thoughts, and making us worry about things more than other people, or making us worry about things that other people don't really worry about. Emphasise that when we think in unhelpful ways, we usually feel unhappy or uncomfortable. Use an example relevant to the young person to assist with illustrating this (try to illustrate with a non-OCD example and then an OCD example).

- The therapist should then **encourage the young person to use helpful thoughts to boss OCD back!** As the young person has just completed an ERP task, the therapist could help them to generate some helpful thoughts to use in relation to this task. It can be particularly helpful to use examples of past successes in beating OCD. For example, 'I just touched the bathroom door and didn't wash my hands afterwards!' (Use examples from the young person's own experiences.)

- Explain to the young person that **sometimes it can be helpful just to let OCD know that you are in control, and wait for the unhelpful thoughts to go away**. If we don't let OCD worry or upset us, eventually the OCD will go away! It can be helpful in using this 'bossing back' strategy to generate a list of four or more coping statements that are relevant for the young person. The following are just some examples:

  - I know you are just OCD.
  - You are just trying to trick me into becoming worried or upset.
  - I don't have to listen to you.
  - I don't have to do what you tell me to do.
  - I am the boss, not you.
  - Go away, OCD.
  - I'm not going to do what you want any more.

- **The therapist should ensure that the young person does not use thoughts or an alternative activity to distract themselves away from feeling anxious when doing an exposure task**. It should be stressed that while doing the exposure the young person should try to remain focused on the anxiety-provoking trigger or thought in order to achieve meaningful habituation. Sometimes it helps for them to keep saying what they have done and what the worry is, for example, 'I have touched the toilet seat and I have got germs on my hands' and to keep saying this until the anxiety comes down.

THERAPIST NOTE

If a young person is really struggling to do any ERP then it is permissible to discuss doing ERP and allowing distraction during the anxious phase to start with – but this must be done explicitly and it must be explained to the young person and family that in time that distraction must be withdrawn for proper habituation to take place. Similarly, it could be negotiated that the young person could do an exposure and then agree to delay the ritual to start with – but ultimately they will need to move on to not doing the ritual at all.

- **Encourage the young person to identify their own 'bossing back' statements** that they can use when OCD is bothering them. See workbook page 46.

THERAPIST NOTE

Sessions with the young person from here will predominantly focus on ERP. Additional tools that may assist with ERP are included later in this manual (see pages 40–44), with accompanying worksheets in the workbook (see page 112). The therapist should use their clinical judgement in deciding whether or not to introduce these tools to the young person. It can be helpful to use these tools to facilitate exposure tasks, or to help to modify a young person's thinking when they seem to be holding on to an obsessional belief very rigidly.

4. Homework discussion for young person
(See workbook page 49)

- The therapist should then work with the young person to identify an **ERP task to do for homework. This could be to continue or build on what has been done in the session. If the therapist feels the young person will progress well, and quickly with this, select another ERP task** for the young person to progress to if they can during the week (see workbook page 47). The therapist should seek to negotiate and collaboratively work with the young person to identify the ERP task. Remind the young person that anxiety is unpleasant in the short term, but it quickly goes away, and it will lead to long-term gain.

- **Use the worksheets in the workbook (pages 47–48) to help the young person set up an exposure task and to monitor anxiety once the exposure task has finished.** These sheets can then also be used as a record of progress with ERP.

- Remember to **guide the young person toward selecting tasks that are towards the lower end of the hierarchy.** It is often helpful to continue to progress along a hierarchy until the overall fear is eliminated (e.g. continue to select contamination fears and rituals until the young person has mastered all contamination fears). Frame the ERP as an opportunity to experiment and see whether OCD is telling the truth. Encourage the young person to complete the ERP process using the monitoring sheets provided, and remind them to remain in the situation until habituation occurs.

- **The therapist should plan with the young person exactly when they are going to engage in their ERP practice.** It is important to set a specific time each day, and to continue to remain in the situation until the anxiety has significantly reduced. Remember that **daily practice is what the young person should be aiming for**.

- The therapist should discuss with the young person any difficulties that they can foresee. For example, are they worried that they won't be able to do this? What else could they do? What, if any, difficulties do they envisage? The therapist should problem-solve through any difficulties with the young person.

- The therapist should **answer any questions that the young person may have**. Also ask the young person to use the homework worksheet to write three things they have learned in Session 3 and any questions that they may have over the course of the week, which will be addressed in the next session.

- **Check with the young person how their parent(s) are doing** in terms of helping the young person. Discuss any issues that may arise (e.g. conflict with parents, young person not wanting help, young person not finding parents' efforts helpful). Explain to the young person that you are now going to have a discussion with their parents.

 Remember to make the next appointment time with the young person.

5. Parent check-in and homework discussion for parents

- The therapist should briefly **review the previous session and homework**. Discuss any issues that may arise.

- **Explain to parents what has been discussed with the young person in this session.** Give parents the opportunity to ask any questions that they may have about the session content (or about OCD in general).

- **Discuss with parents the young person's homework task(s) for this week.**

- **Discuss parents' homework.** If it seems helpful at this point:
  - ask parents to start to think of how the family accommodates OCD. That is, how does OCD boss them or other family members around? What does OCD make the family do that they wouldn't

otherwise do? Encourage the parents to begin to make a list of these situations. If the young person is happy to talk to parents about their OCD, ask the parents and young person to begin to build this list together. Tool 8 covers Reassurance seeking and accommodation of OCD – please refer to page 40 of this manual and pages 112–113 of the workbook for more detail about this

- ask parents to praise the young person for times when they see that the young person is resisting the OCD, or bossing OCD back. This should be each day now, as the young person has been asked to do daily ERP practice if possible.

 Remember to check with parents that the next appointment time is suitable for them.

Sessions 4-6

CONTINUE FIGHTING OCD USING ERP

Sessions 4–6 (and 8–12) are focused largely on ERP and should follow the same basic format. Therefore, an overview of this format will be presented here, and the therapist should introduce various discussion topics with the young person/parent sessions according to clinical need. **The tools contained after Session 14 of this manual (see pages 40–41) can also be used according to clinical need.**

Don't forget to stop and review at Session 7 – the content of which is described in the next session. If the ERP is progressing well, and quickly, there is no need to continue through to Session 12. Relapse prevention can be commenced when the therapist feels that the young person has made significant progress and is ready to look at maintenance of therapeutic gains.

PLAN FOR SESSIONS 4–6: Allow 45–60 minutes

1. Review previous session and homework tasks
2. Carry out in-vivo ERP during session
3. Homework discussion for young person: select an exposure task or tasks for homework
4. Parent check-in and homework discussion for parents

1 Review previous session and review homework

- The therapist should spend some time at the start of the session **reviewing the previous session,** checking that the young person fully understood what was discussed.

- After reviewing the assigned ERP tasks, the therapist should also **ask the young person more broadly about their OCD successes** by asking for other examples of when the young person made OCD wait, or when the young person was able to say 'no' to OCD.

- **The therapist should then review the young person's experience of ERP for homework.** Give plenty of positive reinforcement for the young person's efforts as well as their successes.

- **If the young person was not successful**, the therapist should carefully step through the young person's experience to try and think through the possible reasons for this.

   • Did the young person discontinue ERP too early?

   • Did the young person engage in any rituals or any other neutralising behaviours?

   • Did the young person distract themselves from the experience of anxiety?

   • Did the young person reinforce the OCD by giving in to the fear messages?

   • Was the task simply too difficult for the young person to do on their own without the therapist's support?

If the young person was unsuccessful in the ERP task, normalise this experience for the young person, and let the young person know that you will work together to break down the task or to pick some more appropriate ERP tasks to commence with. The step plans that are included in the workbook (page 54) can be used to break down an OCD symptom into more manageable steps.

- If homework was not completed at all, perhaps just due to the family being too busy, a discussion should be had about the importance of homework and practising ERP every day between sessions otherwise the treatment will not be effective. Then there may need to be some problem-solving around how to make sure that the homework can be done over the following week.

2. Carry out in-vivo ERP during session

(See workbook pages 52-54 for step plans and ERP record forms for monitoring anxiety)

- The young person should now be familiar with the basic process of fighting back against OCD using ERP. **The primary focus of Sessions 4–12 will be on completing in-vivo (within session) ERP tasks together** as well as following up on these for homework. **The homework goal is daily practice.**

- **A note about in-vivo exposure during the session:** It cannot be stressed enough **how important it is to use time during the session to practise ERP tasks with the young person.**

  - Make sure that you **start the process of agreeing and carrying out the task as early as possible** in the session so that there is time for habituation to take place while you are together.

  - Sometimes these tasks require **forward planning**. You may need to ask the young person to **bring a trigger item** to the session or you may need to source some yourself (e.g. images that relate to their intrusive thoughts; items that are considered contaminated).

  - You may need to plan to **carry out the session in the young person's home** or local area if that is the place where OCD is at its most powerful.

  - By practising with them you are first ensuring that they are **carrying out the exposure in the most effective way** possible, helping them to notice or look out for ways that OCD might make them engage in rituals. You are also **showing parents how best to support their young person to do their ERP tasks**. You are most importantly giving the young person the experience of having made a start with that ERP task, which should then make it much easier for the young person to continue to practise this on their own throughout the week.

- Review the process of designing an ERP task with the young person until they can design graded exposure tasks themselves competently (see page 52):

  - Select one target compulsion (what is OCD telling you to do?).

  - Identify what the 'fighting back' task is going to be (the ERP task).

  - Rate the fear or anxiety felt at the idea of resisting OCD (using the 0–10 rating scale).

  - Identify what tools or coping statements or people might be helpful.

  - Complete the exposure, remembering not to engage in any rituals.

  - Rate the anxiety again once the task is finished, with zero minutes on the monitoring form being the time point immediately that task is finished.

  - Don't forget to keep bossing back OCD using helpful thoughts.

  - Monitor anxiety every few minutes until 0 (or a very low level such as 2–3) is reached. Returning to low anxiety is unlikely to take more than 60 minutes at most. Some young people with severe, pervasive OCD report that they rarely, if ever, reach a 0 on their anxiety scale owing to being constantly 'a bit on edge'. If this is the case then it is important to be aware of their usual level of anxiety (probably around 2–3) so that during habituation you know that this is the level you are expecting the young person to return to.

  - Use this task as evidence to boss back OCD in the future tasks.

  - Use the task as an opportunity to consider what the young person has learned: (a) about anxiety, and (b) about the fears or obsession.

- Remember to **collaborate with the young person and select tasks that are toward the lower end of the hierarchy**, progressing upward in a graded way and at the young person's pace. It is often helpful to continue to progress along a hierarchy until the overall fear is eliminated (e.g. continue to select contamination fears and rituals until the young person has mastered all contamination fears). The step plans that are included in the workbook can be used to clearly identify the ERP step that is being targeted.

Therapist notes to assist in designing ERP tasks

- Ensure that the young person understands that ERP tasks are used for avoided situations as well as deliberately targeting situations that usually trigger OCD rituals.

- It is also important to **ensure that the ERP task is engaged in fully**. That is, that the young person is not avoiding anxiety by distracting themselves, mentally ritualising, only doing tasks at times when they feel it is 'okay'. If the young person is looking blank or is unable to talk, this may be an indication of them doing a mental ritual. **The aim of ERP tasks is for the young person to experience anxiety, to learn that anxiety itself is not harmful**, and to experience that anxiety goes away by itself, without having the young person do anything.

- The therapist may need to exercise some creativity in designing ERP tasks for certain fears.
    - For example, for obsessional symptoms without compulsions, the therapist should use explicit exposure to the thoughts or images (e.g. writing out a detailed script of the worry or image, re-creating the image on a page, listening to an internal dialogue over and again). It may also be helpful to make a recording of the obsession in order that it be played back over and again. The therapist should be creative in encouraging the young person to use imaginative visualisation to 'bring to life' the thoughts as vividly as they possibly can.
    - For more guidance on exposure to thoughts go to Tool 9 (page 41 of this manual).

- For some compulsions, it may be necessary to break the compulsion into smaller steps that will allow for graduated ERP. For example, if the compulsion is to wash hands after touching a contaminated object, the young person may be encouraged to 'break the rules' by altering the special way in which they wash their hands. Other strategies for assisting to 'break the rules' include: delaying the ritual; shortening the duration of the ritual; doing the ritual differently; or doing the ritual slowly. But ultimately, the goal should be to resist the ritual altogether in order to beat OCD.

- Forewarn parents that at times the young person might get angry or distressed, and think with parents about how they may manage this. If this does occur, it may be that the assigned task is too difficult for the young person. (To assist in preventing this, the therapist should only assign tasks for homework with the young person's full co-operation, and possibly only after having practised the task during the session with the therapist.)

3 Homework discussion for young person

The therapist should work with the young person to identify an ERP task to do for homework.

- **Homework for these sessions will involve continuing with the ERP tasks outlined** on the young person's step plans. The therapist should encourage the young person to use the monitoring sheets included in the workbook to record their anxiety at the beginning of the task, and to continue to monitor their anxiety as it decreases at the regular time intervals on the sheet.

- Remind the young person that they need to practice ERP each day of the week. Explain that the more we practice bossing back OCD in this way, the easier it becomes for us, and the harder it becomes for the OCD to scare us or make us worries.

- Ask the young person to write any questions that they may have over the course of the week so that these can be addressed in the next session.

 Remember to make the next appointment time with the young person.

4 Parent check-in and homework discussion for parents

- The therapist should briefly **review with parents last week's session and last week's homework tasks**. Discuss any issues that may arise. Review with parents their experiences of any exposure tasks that involve gradual removal of family involvement and accommodation, and discuss any issues that arose. Give parents the opportunity to ask any questions.

- Explain to parents what has been discussed with the young person in this session.

- **Discuss with parents the young person's homework task(s) and the parents' homework task(s).**

- Parents should be encouraged to continue to offer support to their young person, in the form of praise for effort and success, and in the form of an identified reward for the young person's efforts.

- Therapists may feel that it is not necessary to check in with parents every week if the young person is continuing to progress well with their ERP tasks; however, this should be a decision made by the young person and the parents.

 Remember to check with parents that the next appointment time is suitable for them.

Session 7

REVIEW PROGRESS

> **PLAN FOR SESSION 7: Allow 45–60 minutes**
>
> 1. Review previous session and homework task
> 2. Review progress and measure OCD
> 3. Update the OCD hierarchy
> 4. Continue with in-vivo ERP
> 5. Homework discussion for young person
> 6. Parent check-in and homework discussion for parents

1. Review previous session and homework task

- The therapist should **review the previous session** at the start of the session and **review the young person's experience of ERP for homework**. Give plenty of positive reinforcement for the young person's efforts as well as their successes.

2. Review progress and measure OCD

- An important part of CBT is to **measure the change** that is taking place in order to see how you are progressing in treatment.

- To assess treatment response and overall progress, **an OCD measure should be completed at Session 7**.

- The therapist can use the worksheet **to write down the severity scores** at the start of treatment and half-way through treatment; this will help **record any progress** made during the OCD treatment and to emphasise the young person's improvement and success in fighting OCD.

- **If progress is not being made, the following questions may be helpful to consider:**

  - Are there **obsessions not yet revealed** (see Tool 9, page 41 of this manual)?

  - Is the young person **engaging in rituals during ERP** (mental rituals, subtle discreet rituals, self-reassurance, simply delaying rituals) and thus preventing habituation from taking place?

  - Is the young person **managing daily ERP at home** or do they need more support to do this?

  - Are there **other things going on outside this treatment that need to be tackled** first? In which case, better to pause treatment and come back to it at a later time than to continue with no progress.

- If progress is not being made after seven sessions **it is very important to review and work out what is getting in the way of progress**. To continue with treatment that is not working will only serve to discourage both the young person and the therapist as to the efficacy of this approach.

3. Update the OCD hierarchy

- The therapist should spend some time updating the OCD hierarchy that the young person generated at the start of treatment to keep abreast of any changes. For example, are there new symptoms? Are some of the existing symptoms changing or disappearing? Are any of the anxiety ratings changing? (It is common for anxiety ratings and symptoms to change as the young person begins the battle with OCD.)

- If positive changes are noted, **emphasise the young person's successes over the OCD.** If therapy is telephone-based, the therapist should keep their own notes of the young person's OCD hierarchy, and update these each week as well. There is space in the workbook (page 67) to **update the symptom hierarchy**.

4. Continue with in-vivo ERP
(See workbook page 68)

- Session 7 should also allow some time for an in-vivo (within session) ERP task together. More information on setting up and assistance with designing ERP task is provided on pages 24–25 of this manual.

5. Homework discussion for young person
(See workbook page 71)

- The therapist should then work with the young person to **identify an ERP task to do for homework.** This could be to continue what has been done in the session and any other ERP task for the young person to progress to if they can during the week (workbook page 71).

- More details on homework discussion for the young person can be found on pages 25–26 of this therapist manual.

 Remember to make the next appointment time with the young person.

6. Parent check-in and homework discussion for parents

- The therapist should briefly **review with parents last week's session and last week's homework tasks**. Discuss any issues that may arise.

- **Explain to parents what has been discussed with the young person in this session**, including a summary on treatment progress.

- Collect any **OCD measures** that parents were asked to complete.

- Discuss with parents **the young person's homework task(s) and any parents' homework task(s)**. More details on homework discussion can be found on page 25–26 of this manual.

 Remember to check with parents that the next appointment time is suitable for them.

Sessions 8-12

CONTINUE FIGHTING OCD USING ERP

Sessions 8–12 continue to be focused on ERP and should follow the format set out for Sessions 4–6.

> **PLAN FOR SESSIONS 8–12: Allow 45–60 minutes**
>
> 1. Review previous session and homework tasks
> 2. Carry out in-vivo ERP during session
> 3. Homework discussion for young person: select an exposure task or tasks for homework
> 4. Parent check-in and homework discussion for parents

Please see pages 28–31 of this manual for the detailed format of Sessions 8–12.

Session 13

COMPLETING ERP AND OVERLEARNING IN OCD

> **PLAN FOR SESSION 13: Allow 45–60 minutes**
>
> 1. Review Session 12 and homework
> 2. Extending ERP by using overlearning
> 3. Homework discussion for young person
> 4. Parent check-in and homework discussion for parents

1. Review Session 12 and homework

- The therapist should review the previous session and **review the young person's experience of ERP for homework**. Give plenty of positive reinforcement for the young person's efforts as well as their successes.

2. Extending ERP using overlearning
(See workbook page 96)

- The therapist and young person should be close to having completed the ERP, with only a minimal number of symptoms remaining. **Where further progress with ERP is required, the therapist should continue to work with the young person to select which ERP task they will progress to.** Ensure that the young person understands they must continue to **use the ERP and fighting back strategies for any residual symptoms that remain**.

- To complete the ERP, the therapist might like to think together with the young person about overlearning (i.e. some ERP targets that will go beyond their current limit of experience). It is useful to extend ERP in order to be able to prepare for, and where possible prevent, relapse.

- **Overlearning** takes an exposure task beyond the limit of usual experience. It is important and useful to do as a final step in overcoming OCD. An example may help to illustrate how this works in practice. For example, if OCD makes a young person worry about toilet germs, they could place a piece of food on a toilet seat and then eat it. But this would not be something they would be expected to do as part of every day. (It is important to remember with any ERP task that modelling by being prepared to do the task yourself is important!) As the overlearning task is likely just to be a one-off, the emphasis is not so much on habituation but just being brave enough to do it as a victory over OCD. Sometimes young people like to photograph themselves doing an overlearning task as evidence of their achievement in treatment.

- Overlearning may involve **taking a risk** and/or **tolerating uncertainty**. These are two very important things to master if the young person wishes to maintain good recovery from OCD.

- Once the task has been agreed then the therapist and young person should carry this out in the session together if possible (it may require some forward planning if props are needed or the young person needs to visit a particular place to carry it out).

3 Homework discussion for young person

(See workbook page 100)

- For homework, **the young person should be encouraged either to continue with ERP for residual symptoms, or to push the boundaries of OCD by planning ERP tasks that go beyond the symptom as it first presented (i.e. overlearning)**. Remind the young person to use the monitoring sheets to record their progress. It may be helpful to negotiate a specific time of day that the young person should practise, and remind them to practise each day.

- Even though overlearning is likely to be challenging, if the young person is confident in their recovery **it can be a time to have some fun, and getting the family involved in these tasks can work well**. Sometimes the young person is more willing to do the overlearning task than their parents or siblings are! But getting everyone to have a go can show the family what it is like to have to do something that makes them feel a bit uncomfortable – and they are usually prepared to do it in the interests of fighting OCD.

- Ask the young person to **write any questions** that they may have over the course of the week so that these can be addressed in the next session.

 Remember to make the next appointment time with the young person.

4 Parent check-in and homework discussion for parents

- The therapist should briefly **review the previous session and homework** with parents. Discuss any issues that may arise.

- **Explain to parents what has been discussed** with the young person in this session. Give parents the opportunity to ask any questions that they may have about the session content or about overlearning.

- Discuss with parents the young person's **homework task(s) for this week**.

- Ask parents to think of any questions that they may like to ask next week, either about their young person's future, and the future of OCD, or any other questions at all.

 Remember to check with parents that the next appointment time is suitable for them.

Session 14

RELAPSE PREVENTION AND END OF WEEKLY TREATMENT SESSIONS

> **PLAN FOR SESSION 14: Allow 60–90 minutes**
>
> You might want to allow up to 90 minutes for this session as there is quite a lot to get through with re-measuring OCD and making a detailed relapse prevention plan.
>
> 1. Review homework and review all that has been discussed/achieved, including a re-measure of OCD
> 2. Continue fighting back: completing ERP and overlearning tasks
> 3. Discussion of relapse prevention
> 4. Introduce the young person to the next tool they will use for fighting OCD
>   **Tool 7:** A relapse prevention plan
> 5. Homework discussion for young person
> 6. Parent check-in and homework discussion for parents

1 Review homework and review all that has been discussed/achieved

- The therapist should review the young person's experiences with ERP since the last session. **Remind the young person that they should continue to use ERP for any residual symptoms and to 'push the boundaries' of OCD (i.e. overlearning).**

- The therapist should then **initiate a major review of the intervention.** The therapist should have all their notes on OCD hierarchies, step plans and progress so that a clear progress update can be done. This should include discussion of:
    - what the young person has learned
    - how the young person thinks they have progressed
    - how the therapist thinks they have progressed
    - how the young person felt about the intervention
    - what the young person liked/did not like
    - what was the most helpful/least helpful.

- Ask the young person to write down in the worksheet the five most important things they learned in CBT to fight OCD. Use the following questions to facilitate your discussion: How did my OCD start? What kept it going? What did I learn in therapy? What strategies have I learned that I wouldn't want to ever forget? What are my goals for the future? What will help me to achieve these goals?

- Give plenty of positive reinforcement and encouragement for the young person's efforts throughout therapy, and ensure that they take 'ownership' of their successes.

2 Continue fighting back: completing ERP and overlearning tasks

- It is important to emphasise that while CBT sessions are coming to an end, the young person will need to **keep fighting OCD**.

- Encourage the young person to **set some ERP tasks to complete during the course of the month**, until your next appointment. The therapist might like to think together with the young person about some ERP targets that will go beyond their current limit of experience. It is useful to extend ERP in order to be able to prepare for, and where possible, prevent relapse.

3 Discussion of relapse prevention

- The therapist should **explain what relapse prevention is**. The therapist should discuss with the young person that although they have achieved significant progress, **OCD may try to come back into the young person's life**. Explain that this is normal, and indeed often expected in the course of the young person's fight against OCD. Emphasise, however, that these **lapses are often minor, and can be managed quickly and easily by the young person and family** if they have a plan of action. The young person may want to use their own words for talking about relapse prevention — some people use words like 'minor set-backs' or a 'blip', and if so, the therapist should adopt their language.

- It can actually be helpful for the young person to experience a minor relapse while they are still in follow-up, as this is then an opportunity for them to practise their relapse prevention plan and build up their confidence about facing possible set-backs in the future. So, emphasise that relapses should not be feared but used as opportunities to get stronger against OCD.

- OCD is sometimes known to try and come back into a young person's life when new or difficult (stressful) situations arise. In order to plan ahead, the young person should be encouraged to look ahead and identify any possible situations that might be stressful (include positive stressors here as well). Some examples include changing school/going to college, moving house, a new young person in the family, death of a pet or loved one, exams, conflict at home, conflict with friends and in relationships, and so on. See workbook page 105.

4 Introduce the young person to the next tool they will use for fighting OCD

Tool 7: A relapse prevention plan
(See workbook page 107)

- **Help the young person to formulate a plan for managing potential lapses** when/if they occur. The therapist should lead the young person toward the following ideas:

  - **Recognising OCD.** What might be the early warning signs that OCD is trying to sneak back in? What might it look like/feel like (e.g. moody, feeling uncomfortable/upset, wanting to withdraw from other people)?

  - What is the **symptom cluster(s)** that is (are) most likely to return? Why?

  - Who may else may notice OCD symptoms coming back?

  - **Act early** (don't avoid tackling OCD — it is easiest to beat when it is caught early).

  - Mobilise a **support team** (e.g. discuss with parents or another trusted person what has happened).

  - **Develop an action plan** (use the tools learned already to fight back against OCD and remind the young person that an action plan should definitely include ERP). The action plan should also include an action plan for parents.

  - **Overlearning:** when OCD has been tackled, do additional ERP activities to go above and beyond the fear (continue to develop strength).

  - **Tell someone** and **decide when to seek extra help** from a therapist, if required.

- Encourage the young person to think of how **parents might help** in the event that a lapse should occur. Suggest that parents are often especially helpful in identifying OCD when it reappears (sometimes even before the young person may notice that OCD is there). Discuss with the young person that it is important to remain open to feedback from parents, because they may notice things that the young person didn't notice. (If possible, try and obtain an example from the young person's own experiences of where parents noticed something that at first the young person did not.) If the young person is unable to identify such an example, the therapist may like to share an example of their own. For example, when I am feeling tired or stressed at work, I may become more irritable than usual. Although I don't notice it, my family might point out that I am more irritable than usual and they might ask me if something is wrong.

- If the young person has been taking **medication**, be sure to include in the discussion the withdrawal of medication as a possible time when OCD might lapse. It is by no means certain that this would occur, but some young people do report a slight increase in OCD symptoms at this stage (remember, many don't!). The therapist should emphasise to the young person that this is normal; however, it does not mean that the medication has been responsible for the symptom reduction. Stress to the young person that they have done all the hard work in learning to overcome and manage OCD.

- **It is usually recommended that a young person should remain on SSRI (selective serotonin reuptake inhibitor) medication for 6–12 months after recovery from OCD.** Medication withdrawal should always be overseen by an experienced child psychiatrist.

5 Homework discussion for young person

- For homework, the young person should be encouraged either to **continue with ERP for residual symptoms, or for overlearning**.

- **Praise the young person for their continued efforts** and congratulate them on their achievements.

Follow-up sessions

- The therapist should discuss the follow-up sessions offered to the young person. These are scheduled at one month, three months, six months, and then again 12 months after the completion of the weekly sessions.

 Make a date and time with the young person for the first follow-up session.

6 Parent check-in and homework discussion for parents

- The parent check-in and discussion should focus on any questions that they might have, and on ensuring that the **family have an adequate set-back plan**.

- Discuss the **schedule for follow-up sessions** as above and remind parents that follow-up evaluations will occur.

- **Thank the parent** for their continued support of their young person and for the gains and achievements made by the family.

 Remember to check with parents that the next appointment time is suitable for them.

ADDITIONAL TOOLS FOR FIGHTING OCD

Notes for therapists on Tools 8-12

- During Sessions 4–13, the majority of the time will be spent focusing on Tool 5: Exposure and response prevention (ERP), both during the sessions (in vivo) and as part of the session, planning and reviewing the ERP tasks carried out for daily homework practice.

- Tools 1–7 listed below are the **essential tools** needed for treating all young people with OCD and will equip both therapist and young person with all or most of what they need to carry out ERP, fight their OCD and achieve a good recovery:
    - Tool 1: Externalising OCD
    - Tool 2: Understanding anxiety
    - Tool 3: Making an OCD hierarchy
    - Tool 4: The OCD cycle
    - Tool 5: Exposure and response prevention
    - Tool 6: Bossing back OCD using helpful thoughts
    - Tool 7: A relapse prevention plan.

- Tools 8–12 listed below will **not necessarily be relevant for all young people** but the notes in this section will tell you more about these tools and when you might consider using them. Tools 8–12 are placed in the workbook at the end of the weekly sessions and before the follow-up sessions. Tools 8, 9 and 10 are the most commonly used of these additional tools and there is reference to them early on in the workbook that may prompt the therapist and young person to refer to them:
    - Tool 8: Reassurance seeking and accommodation of OCD
    - Tool 9: Normalising intrusive thoughts
    - Tool 10: Learning to let thoughts go
    - Tool 11: Responsibility pie charts
    - Tool 12: Don't believe OCD – find out for yourself!

Tool 8: Reassurance seeking and accommodation of OCD
(See workbook pages 112-113)

- It is **very common in OCD for the young person to involve family members in their OCD** either by asking them questions, seeking reassurance from them over a whole range of issues (e.g. Are things clean? Am I a paedophile? Will everyone be okay?) and by getting them to do things for OCD. Parents and siblings can find themselves having to take showers when they don't want to, avoiding touching things themselves so as not to upset the young person, preparing food in a special way, avoiding watching certain things on TV, avoiding saying certain things or having to say things a certain way, and so on. In effect, the family can be acting as if they have OCD themselves in order to accommodate the young person's OCD.

- In order to tackle this in treatment, the first thing is to ensure that the young person and family **recognise that these behaviours are part of OCD** and something that needs to be addressed and changed as part of effective treatment. Ensure that all the OCD rituals which involve the family are included in the young person's OCD hierarchy.

- The workbook prompts the family to identify specific ways in which the young person may be **asking for reassurance** and then suggests different ways that the family might respond to these questions. Encourage the young person and parent to discuss exactly what will happen when the young person seeks reassurance. For example, parents could give general encouragement to the young person for fighting OCD rather than answering the questions, or respond with a particular statement (e.g. I know OCD would like me to answer that question for you, but we know that will not help us. We agreed that I would not answer these questions this week. Well done for trying so hard.).

- If getting reassurance is very high up on the OCD hierarchy and the young person would be extremely anxious (e.g. 8–10 on the anxiety rating scale) if not receiving reassurance, then it is managed in the same way as all other compulsions. That is, it **may need to be**

broken down into more manageable steps.
For example:

- Step 1 could involve **rationing the reassurance** given to a certain number of questions per day, or at certain times of the day for a set period.

- Step 2 could be to respond with a **set answer** as suggested above and in the workbook.

- Step 3 may be to **ignore** the reassurance seeking altogether and just not say anything at all.

- Step 4 could be to **say the opposite** of what OCD wants to hear, for instance, 'Maybe something bad *will* happen to me when I go out'. This step might align best to the later stages of treatment, when the young person has grasped the idea of doing the opposite of what OCD wants and doing more extreme exposure tasks.

Role play

- It can be very helpful for the therapist to role-play these responses with the young person and the family in preparation for the family trying them out at home when anxiety may be running high. This can be done in a variety of ways – if the young person is willing to join in, then the therapist can role-play the parent as a way of demonstrating to the parent how to respond clearly and calmly. The parent could also role-play being the young person and really show the therapist how persistent the young person might be if they are anxious. Finally, you could even ask the young person to role-play being the parent and not giving reassurance as a way of the young person showing that they understand what their parent is being asked to do and how hard it might be for them at times.

- In our experience, once the young person knows the importance of their parents not giving reassurance, then they are often the ones who will pick their parents up on it!

- All the same principles can be used when reducing the things that the family are doing for OCD (**accommodation of OCD**). First, it is essential to discuss this openly with the young person so that they know, and ideally are in agreement, that the parent is going to stop doing these things for OCD. If stopping altogether is too anxiety-provoking, then breaking the accommodating tasks down into smaller steps would again be the approach to take.

- Supporting the family to stop accommodating OCD can sometimes be the most challenging part of treating OCD in young people. It may need a great deal of work to get everyone involved to understand how their behaviour is reinforcing and maintaining the young person's difficulties, and therefore to help them to stop these behaviours. The young person with OCD is often very resistant to the idea of their family not doing these things any more and may not collaborate in the planning to reduce accommodating behaviour.

- In this situation, it might be helpful to offer parents the opportunity to have sessions alone, in the young person's knowledge, to **work on reducing accommodation of OCD even if the young person is not in agreement**. This is far from ideal, but is sometimes the only way for a parent or family to start freeing themselves from the burden that OCD has become in their own lives. There are two possible outcomes of this approach. The best-case scenario is that the young person copes well with the gradual reduction in family accommodation and learns that it is okay to go against what OCD says, thereby improving their OCD. Of course, the other scenario is that the young person struggles to deal with their OCD as family members withdraw from rituals, and their OCD becomes worse. This will either prompt the young person to realise that they cannot continue like this and to be more willing to engage in treatment, but it is also possible that this may trigger a crisis and in severe cases, can even lead to hospital admission.

- It is crucial that these possible outcomes are considered and explicitly discussed with parents before embarking on graded reduction of family accommodation without the young person's agreement. Some parents may not feel it is the right time to take this step. However, many parents feel that doing 'something' is better than doing nothing and allowing the situation to continue as it is, especially if the family and young person's lives have been devastated by OCD.

Tool 9: Normalising intrusive thoughts
(See workbook page 114)

- It is very common for young people with OCD to experience extremely disturbing intrusive thoughts about terrible things happening and particularly about themselves doing terrible things to others. These would usually become evident when assessing the young person, for example, in completing a CY-BOCS assessment and inquiring about aggressive and sexual obsessions.

- However, sometimes the young person is so upset, embarrassed and fearful about these thoughts, and about speaking them aloud, that they hide them from the therapist and their family. This can be **a common reason why treatment fails – when the real fear has not been spoken about** – so it is helpful to keep this in mind if you suspect that a young person has not fully revealed all of their obsessions to you. Tool 9 could help you to discuss this with them, if they have not yet spoken about this. Tool 9 will also be an essential part of their treatment if distressing, intrusive thoughts are clearly part of their OCD presentation.

- The first part of this tool in the workbook (pages 114–115) makes the point that **intrusive thoughts are entirely normal and everyone experiences them**. It then goes on to distinguish between **positive, neutral and negative intrusive thoughts** and refers to a survey that illustrates how common it is for people to have unpleasant, bizarre or even taboo thoughts. The full survey results are available in the following publication and may be therapeutic to share with some young people who are experiencing disturbing intrusive thoughts as part of their OCD: Purdon C. and Clark D. (1992) 'Obsessive intrusive thoughts in nonclinical subjects. Part 1. Content & relation with depressive, anxious and obsessional symptoms.' *Behaviour Research and Therapy*, 31, 713–720. In our experience, the sharing of this information about thoughts can often be a huge relief to young people who, up until this point, may have attached terrible meaning to their experience of having these thoughts. This process may also lead to further disclosure of obsessional thoughts; for example, the young person may feel able to say that they experience intrusive thoughts similar to some of those listed in the survey.

- The next part of the tool goes on to discuss the **specific nature of intrusive thoughts in OCD**. Having established that the occurrence of these thoughts is normal, the young person then needs to understand that it is **the meaning that they attach to them and the behaviour they feel compelled to do in response** that turns these thoughts from fleeting, normal, slightly unsettling thoughts into obsessional symptoms of OCD.

- The workbook addresses the issue of how powerful OCD can make thoughts seem. **Thought-action fusion** is a very common 'trick' in OCD; for example, people with OCD sometimes think:
  - because I have a thought about something, this means that it will happen or at least is more likely to happen
  - because I have a thought about something awful, this means that I am a bad person (perhaps because thinking something awful is almost as bad as doing something awful, and/or it means that I want this awful thing to happen).

- Once a young person appreciates that the way they feel about these thoughts is all part of an OCD trick, then they are sometimes more willing to begin the process of tackling this part of their OCD.

- We recommend that intrusive thoughts in OCD are tackled in just the same way as compulsions; that is, by using ERP. Young people will avoid these thoughts and anything that triggers them and they will do extensive rituals to try to bring down the anxiety associated with them. Therefore, the approach should be as follows:
  - Reveal the content and detail of all intrusive thoughts, if possible. Revealing the content and detail of thoughts will be an exposure in itself, so it may need to be done **in a graded way**. For example, write the thoughts down, speak them out, reveal them partially at the outset, and then in more detail later.
  - Once the content of the thoughts is understood, then exposure tasks can be planned in line with this.
  - The workbook makes suggestions for how to tackle exposure to the thoughts directly through **deliberately thinking about them, listening to them on audio voice recordings**, and so on.
  - There may also be some useful work done through **exposure to triggers**; for example, if a young person is having thoughts that they might kill their mother then ultimately a task might be to hold a sharp knife to her throat while saying 'I want to kill you'. We realise that this sounds extreme, but it is important to note that this is the image that OCD has been putting into the young person's head for weeks and weeks and this is just a way of facing it and helping the young person to realise that once they face it repeatedly, the power and anxiety goes out of it over time.
  - To give another example, if a young person reports **paedophilic obsessions**, exposure may involve deliberately looking

at pictures of children (which they would otherwise probably avoid) while deliberately bringing on the thoughts that OCD is making them think, such as 'What if I am a paedophile? Maybe I am a bad person who wants to do terrible things to children.'

- Sometimes therapists feel anxious about carrying out these kind of exposure tasks with 'taboo' obsessions, and they worry that it may be risky. **It is crucial to keep in mind that people with OCD do not act out their obsessional thoughts – these thoughts represent their greatest fears.**

- In all of these exposure tasks, remind the young person about **response prevention.** Common responses to intrusive thoughts are neutralising, replacing the bad thought with a good one, mental rituals, prayer rituals, repeatedly apologising, and so on. It is essential that the young person is supported to **resist engaging in rituals while doing exposure to thoughts** in order for the ERP to be effective.

Tool 10: Learning to let thoughts go
(See workbook page 119)

- For young people who experience distressing thoughts as part of their OCD, Tool 9 will help them to address these through normalising these thoughts and tackling them with exposure and response prevention (Tool 5).

- Once they have spent time completing ERP for these thoughts, the anxiety associated with them should reduce. However, the young person may report that these thoughts continue to pop into their head from time to time.

- Without the extreme distress, it is hoped that these obsessions are now not interfering, although they can be annoying and at times still distressing. It is important for the therapist to emphasise that **this is normal.** Obsessional thoughts may continue to pop into mind for some time yet. They may always come and go, with no predictability to them, or they may continue to slowly disappear as the young person learns to become more and more confident in fighting OCD.

- The goal for such **'residual thoughts' is to allow them to come and go**, in the same way in which most other thoughts come and go in our mind without us becoming too distressed by them, and even without us noticing them too much. In our experience, it is difficult for a young person to achieve this unless the anxiety associated with such intrusive thoughts is at a low level (usually in the later stages of treatment). If anxiety remains moderate to high, then further ERP work is likely to be required.

- When anxiety is low, then the young person can be encouraged to ignore the intrusive thoughts, not react to them, and just carry on doing whatever it was that they were doing when the thought arrived. The workbook gives some ideas as to how to do this. It is important to emphasise that the thought should not be pushed away, or avoided, or followed by any other kind of distraction or neutralisation.

- The ultimate goal is to **DO NOTHING** when these thoughts pop into the mind.

- This concept is referred to as 'cultivating detachment' and was popularised by Jeff Schwartz in his book *Brain Lock* (1996).

Tool 11: Responsibility pie charts
(See workbook page 120)

- Many young people feel that **if something dreadful happens, it is their fault**. For example, OCD might say that if the young person does not wash their hands after touching taps with germs on them, it will be their fault if Mum or Dad gets sick. To apply real reasoning to this fear, the therapist should encourage the young person to brainstorm a list of possible factors that might contribute to the feared event happening. Make sure to place the young person being responsible at the end of the list.

- Then, draw a pie chart to brainstorm together **what approximate percentage of responsibility might be assigned to each of the factors listed**. The young person is asked at the final step to assign the percentage of responsibility that they might have in the outcome actually occurring. By working through this process, the young person is able to boss back OCD by rightly asserting that OCD is trying to trick them into feeling overly responsible for something that is not their fault.

- The therapist should then try and relate this strategy to the young person's own experience of OCD. Help the young person to think of a worry that they have **where OCD is inflating their sense of responsibility**. Help the young person to fight back against the

OCD worry by using real reasoning. Have the young person brainstorm some of the 'real' reasons for why this might happen. Then ask the young person to assign a 'percentage of responsibility' to each reason. Finally, ask them how much they would be to blame if the outcome did occur? Highlight that this is **another way that OCD tricks us into worrying about things,** and now we have a tool for fighting back!

- Ideally, the use of real reasoning strategies will be followed up with ERP tasks to cement the learning.

Tool 12: Don't believe OCD – find out for yourself!
(See workbook pages 123-124)

- As therapists, we are well aware of the fact that **obsessional thoughts and compulsive behaviours are irrational**. In other words, people with OCD are worried about things that won't actually happen or are very unlikely to happen, and they carry out unnecessary rituals. Most people with OCD have insight, which means that they also recognise that their thoughts are irrational and that their rituals are excessive. They might say, 'I know it sounds silly, but I keep worrying about [x, y, z]', or 'I know I don't really need to, but for some reason I can't stop doing [x, y, z]'. However, this is not always the case, and **some young people are convinced that their fear is very much grounded in reality and that their rituals are necessary.** In these cases, it can be helpful to challenge these beliefs by fact-finding.

- The workbook outlines two strategies for fact-finding. The first is **doing some research**. This is most likely to be helpful **in cases where the young person lacks insight into the irrationality of their obsessional fear**. The example given in the workbook is a young person who believes that urine is poisonous. Rather than just telling the young person that this isn't the case, it can be much more powerful to ask them to do some research and find out for themselves. This can be done in the session or in between sessions as homework. Either way, the therapist can aid this process by helping the young person to plan how they will do their research. For example, if they are using the internet, help them to think about what search terms they will use and identify which websites they will look at. The goal here is for the young person to find evidence that their obsessional fear is irrational from a **credible source**. Of course, this kind of fact-finding will not be a magic solution and just because, for example, the young person finds out that urine is not poisonous, it will not automatically mean that they stop worrying about it. However, fact-finding may help to give them confidence to embark on ERP or to push ERP tasks to the next level.

- The second fact-finding strategy is **carrying out surveys**. This is most often useful when the young person **lacks insight into the excessive nature of their rituals**. In other words, they think that their rituals are normal and reasonable. The example given in the workbook is excessive handwashing. Some young people, particularly if they have suffered from OCD for a very long time, **may have lost sight of what is normal** and genuinely believe that it is perfectly reasonable to spend ten minutes scrubbing their hands after going to the toilet. In such cases, it can be helpful to challenge their belief by asking other people what they do in a survey. The workbook gives an example of questions that might be included in a survey of handwashing and also suggests factors to consider before carrying out the survey. As with the previous strategy of doing research, surveys will not be a magic solution and just because the young person finds out, for example, that other people spend ten seconds as opposed to ten minutes washing their hands, it will not necessarily mean that they can drop their handwashing ritual just like that. However, as before, it may give them the confidence and motivation they need to start to work on reducing their ritual using ERP techniques.

- To summarise, in some cases **fact-finding can be helpful to increase insight and provide a springboard into ERP. However, be careful that fact-finding does not turn into reassurance.** It is important to distinguish assurance from *re*assurance. Assurance is providing useful information as a one-off, in order to challenge unhelpful beliefs. In contrast, reassurance is when this information is being used repeatedly in order to reduce anxiety. For example, the young person might keep repeating the new-found information in their head (e.g. 'urine is sterile') or keep asking you or other people to repeat it to them. In some cases, the young person might want to keep doing more and more research or more surveys, often striving for a guarantee or certainty that their feared outcome will not occur. In such cases, the therapist should address this directly with the young person, and label this process of reassurance seeking as a new ritual that needs to be tackled just like any other (see Tool 8).

Follow-up Sessions 1-4

Some services are set up to offer blocks of short-term treatment and do not offer longer-term follow-up as standard. However, it is highly recommended and part of the National Institute for Health and Care Excellence guidelines for treatment of OCD that the young person is reviewed for 12 months following treatment. Because OCD is a waxing and waning condition that can re-emerge at times of stress, it is vital in the event of a relapse to get on top of it quickly and this can often be done more easily if the young person is able to check in with their therapist in the 12-month period following treatment.

Four follow-up sessions are to be scheduled following the end of the 14 weekly sessions that were completed. The timescale for these sessions is as follows:

- Follow-up Session 1: one month after the end of weekly sessions

- Follow-up Session 2: three months after the end of weekly sessions

- Follow-up Session 3: six months after the end of weekly sessions

- Follow-up Session 4: 12 months after the end of weekly sessions.

The agenda for each follow-up session is the same. The page numbers referred to in the following pages relate to workbook Follow-Up Session 1 pages. Subsequent follow-up sessions have the same content but page numbers will obviously differ. Note that in our clinic we measure OCD at three-, six- and 12-month follow-up appointments but not at the one month follow-up.

PLAN FOR FOLLOW-UP SESSIONS

1. General review, review of homework and review of current OCD symptoms
2. Action plan to include ERP task for residual symptoms (consider in-vivo ERP and overlearning tasks)
3. Review of relapse prevention plan and adjust for upcoming life events
4. Homework discussion for young person
5. Parent check-in and homework discussion for parents

1. General review, review of homework and review of current OCD symptoms

(See workbook page 126)

- Find out how the young person has got on generally since you last met – life in general and OCD specifically.

- At the end of the previous session, the young person was asked to continue with ERP for any residual OCD symptoms and/or to undertake an overlearning task. The therapist should **review the young person's experiences with these tasks specifically, and with OCD more generally since the last session**. Essentially, this gives the young person the opportunity to show off how well they have been able to maintain the gains they made. The therapist should specifically encourage the young person to reflect on their successes with OCD.

- Some young people may have found it easy to maintain their control over OCD, whereas others may still have some work to do, or they may be finding that fighting OCD is an ongoing struggle. **The therapist should probe for what went well for the young person, and what tools they found helpful in fighting OCD.** Emphasise the young person's skills and experience in being able to fight OCD.

- The therapist should **encourage the young person to take ownership of successes in**

fighting OCD rather than having the young person attribute success to the therapist, to medication or to another possible external cause.

- The therapist should **review what (if any) ongoing symptoms the young person has. This can be done in a variety of ways, for example by either using a CY-BOCS questionnaire**, reviewing their previous OCD list or simply engaging in a general discussion of the young person's typical day. At three-, six- and 12-month follow-ups we would recommend a more detailed review using whichever measure was used at the start, middle and end of treatment.

2 Action plan to include ERP task for residual symptoms (consider in-vivo ERP and overlearning tasks)

(See workbook page 127)

- The therapist should encourage the young person to take control of planning what might be required for overcoming any residual OCD symptoms.

- The young person should now understand that ERP tasks are required to successfully overcome OCD, and they should be able to plan their own ERP tasks. The therapist should guide them in being able to do this successfully. The workbook provides a few prompt questions to help the young person plan what to do with residual symptoms:
  - What sort of exposure and response prevention tasks would be helpful?
  - What tools do you need to help you?
  - Do you need other people to help? What can their role be?
  - When are you going to do these tasks?
  - How often are you going to do them?

- Encourage in-vivo ERP if this is feasible and realistic.

- Encourage the young person to plan an overlearning task if this is possible, and if the timing is right for this.

- **Remind the young person that they should continue to use ERP for any residual** symptoms and to 'push the boundaries' of OCD (i.e. overlearning) following this session.

3 Review of relapse prevention plan and adjust for upcoming life events

(See workbook page 128)

- **Collaboratively review the young person's relapse prevention plans.** The therapist should ensure that the plans are sufficiently detailed in order to allow the young person to be fully prepared for coping with a set-back.

- **Think with the young person about upcoming events in their life that may be difficult or stressful** (e.g. exams, moving school, changes of any kind). Reiterate that these are the times when OCD is most likely to try to sneak back in. Encourage the young person to watch out for symptoms returning, and immediately implement relapse prevention plans if this happens.

- The therapist should discuss the young person's **future goals**, and ensure that they have some ideas of how they might go about achieving their goals.

- The therapist should **be optimistic about the young person being able to remain symptom free, or in control of the OCD symptoms if they should re-occur.**

4 Homework discussion with young person

- For homework, the young person should be encouraged either to continue with ERP for residual symptoms, or for overlearning.

- **Encourage the young person to continue to be prepared for set-backs by spending some time occasionally imagining a set-back experience.**

- Praise the young person for their continued efforts and congratulate them on their achievements.

Plan the dates for the remaining follow-up sessions with the young person.

5 Parent check-in and homework discussion for parents

- The parent check-in and discussion should focus on any questions that they might have, and on helping the family to feel confident that they have a plan in place for dealing with any residual symptoms. Encourage the family to remain positive about the young person's progress and change.

- Answer any questions the parents have about what happens from here (i.e. further follow-up sessions), and encourage the family to feel confident in their knowledge about how to continue to fight OCD.

- Ensure that the **family have an adequate set-back plan** and that the young person and parents are in agreement about their role in helping the young person deal with set-backs.

- **Check the date of future follow-up sessions with parents** and remind parents about the schedule for follow-up assessments.

- **Thank the parent** for their continued support of their young person and for the gains and achievements made by the family.

 Remember to check with parents that the next appointment time is suitable for them.

OCD – Tools to Help You Fight Back!
A CBT Workbook for Young People

Cynthia Turner, Georgina Krebs and Chloë Volz
Illustrated by Lisa Jo Robinson

Paperback: £18.99 / $26.95
ISBN: 978 1 84905 402 7
eISBN: 978 0 85700 770 4
144 pages

Obsessive compulsive disorder (OCD) affects approximately one in a hundred young people, and often makes it difficult to lead happy and productive lives.

Structured as a flexible 14-session programme, this workbook is intended to be used in conjunction with the clinical manual for this title, *OCD – Tools to Help Young People Fight Back!* It sets out an evidence-based treatment for young people with OCD using cognitive behavioural therapy and exposure and response prevention techniques. Designed to be employed in a clinical setting, it uses simple diagrams and illustrations to explain ways to cope with OCD thoughts and behaviours, and provides activities for use both within sessions and at home. The fun and engaging way in which the exercises are designed will encourage the patient to fully involve themselves in the recovery process and overcome their OCD.

An essential resource for clinicians treating young people affected by OCD, this workbook brings together the patient, the therapist and the patient's family to fight OCD as a team.

Dr Cynthia Turner is a Psychologist who holds Honorary Lecturer positions at the University of Queensland and the Institute of Psychiatry at Kings College London, and is an Honorary Consultant Clinical Psychologist at the Maudsley.

Chloë Volz is a Consultant Clinical Psychologist and Team Lead at the National and Specialist OCD, BDD and Related Disorders Service at the Maudsley Hospital, UK where she has worked since 2002.

Georgina Krebs holds a Clinical Research Training Fellowship at the Institute of Psychiatry, Psychology and Neuroscience and is an Honorary Principal Clinical Psychologist at the OCD, BDD and Related Disorders Service at the Maudsley Hospital.